A Matter of Style

A Matter of Style

A practical guide for GCSE and A-level students

O. M. Thomson
MA (Cantab.), BA (Lond.)

Stanley Thornes (Publishers) Ltd

First published in 1973 by Hutchinson Education
Reprinted 1977, 1978
Second edition published in 1982 by Hutchinson Education
Reprinted 1983, 1984, 1985, 1987

Third edition published in 1992 by
Stanley Thornes (Publishers) Ltd
Old Station Drive
Leckhampton
CHELTENHAM GL53 0DN
England

A catalogue record for this book is available from the British Library.

Photoset by Northern Phototypesetting Co, Ltd, Bolton, Lancashire.
Printed and bound in Great Britain at The Bath Press, Avon.

Contents

Foreword

I just adored this film. . . . Her books have got a lot of power. . . . The mountains looked really lovely. . . . One of the best programmes is when the puppets come on. . . . Things like this make the play very thrilling and exciting. . . . This poem has got a marvellous rhythm to it. . . . Romeo had one bit of awful luck. . . . Lady Macbeth was definitely a courageous woman. . . . Catherine loved Heathcliff very much, and this comes over to the reader.

Every teacher of English will recognise the faults of style contained in the above sentences, for they have a way of turning up, in one form or another, every time students hand in their written work. In the first part of this book I have set them out and I have tried to explain the nature of each one of them in a common-sense but not-too-academic manner.

In the second part I draw the students' attention to some of the ways in which various authors write, for example: Somerset Maugham, William Golding and Daphne du Maurier. Short passages are quoted, and certain devices of style and technique, which students will be likely to find useful, are singled out and examined.

1 Short sentences

Short sentences demand complete clarity of thought. They cannot be written without it. Long sentences, on the other hand, because they can so easily become shapeless and disorganized, and be badly written, provide an excuse for avoiding it. That is why some students go in for long sentences and avoid short ones. Of course they do not reason it out like that: instead – if they think about it at all – they decide that short sentences sound abrupt, or immature, or too simple, and that long ones sound impressive. No student who clings to that idea will ever improve. For it is not only a mistake: it is also an excuse for avoiding the labour of thinking clearly.

Short sentences are splendid. They do not sound immature. On the contrary, they give an impression of clarity and strength. Sometimes their presence in a piece of writing produces a fine effect of dignified simplicity. Consider, for example, this passage from *The Glory that was Greece*, by J. C. Stobart:

> The Mediterranean is a sheltered sea. Chains of islands, like stepping stones, invite the timid mariner to venture across it. He can sail from Greece to Asia without losing sight of land. On the west it is not so. Greece and Italy turn their backs on one another. Their neighbouring coasts are the harbourless ones.

A student will do well to write plenty of short sentences. His writing will be better because it has them in it, scattered through it, giving it variety and clarifying the thought.

Now here are some passages which you can invigorate by

re-shaping them in such a way that they include some short sentences. First, rewrite this passage so as to divide it into three sentences, of which the last two are short:

> The school Vanessa attended for the next two years was run in a strict but kindly manner by an elderly parson, and she loved it, because the discipline gave her a sense of security.

Now divide this passage into three sentences, using only twelve words:

> He tapped on the window, but there was no answer and so he tapped again.

Divide this into three sentences, using only four words for the third one:

> There is a moment's pause and then, in a quiet voice, Macduff asks Macbeth why he killed the grooms, showing that he is already suspicious.

Divide this passage into four sentences, instead of two, using only three words for the last one:

> Hardy's poetry is quite different from Wordsworth's, being more detailed and closer to nature. Wordsworth, who regarded himself as a philosopher as well as a poet, is often pretentious, but Hardy never is.

2 *Long sentences*

A *good* long sentence is a unity. Its different parts are so closely related that if a break were made between them it would disturb the flow of thought.

> Suddenly I put my hand upon my mother's arm, for I had heard, in the silent, frosty air, a sound that brought my heart into my mouth – the tap-tapping of the blind man's stick upon the frozen road. (From *Treasure Island*)

Some long sentences are not unities at all: they are long simply because a number of separate statements, which should have had a sentence each, have been bundled together.

> I looked out of the window to see what the weather was like and because it was fine I grabbed hold of my fishing-rod, ran out of the door and started hurrying across the fields towards the river.

Never write a sentence like that one. Whenever you have completed a clear-cut self-contained statement, no matter how short it is, stop. Never put a conjunction at the end of it, instead of a full stop, and run straight through into what should be a new sentence. If you do, you will succeed in writing a sentence that is long simply because it is bad – like the one that has just been quoted. It should have been three sentences:

> I looked out of the window to see what the weather was like. It was fine. So I grabbed hold of my fishing-rod, ran out of the door and started hurrying across the fields towards the river.

Here are some more examples:

> The most exciting holiday I ever had was a Mediterranean cruise and it lasted two months.

> The most exciting holiday I ever had was a Mediterranean cruise. It lasted two months.

> *David Copperfield* is filled with all sorts of strange characters, and perhaps the most fascinating one of all is Uriah Heep.

> *David Copperfield* is filled with all sorts of strange characters. Perhaps the most fascinating one of all is Uriah Heep.

> They had no sympathy for her but criticized the untidiness of the kitchen and complained that the towels were dirty.

> They had no sympathy for her. They criticized the untidiness of the kitchen and complained that the towels were dirty.

It is equally bad to join together two separate statements by using a participle (which is a word that ends in *-ing*):

> The boy was horrified by the thought of what he had done, being so unnerved by it that he did not dare to go back into the room.

> The boy was horrified by the thought of what he had done. He was so unnerved by it that he did not dare to go back into the room.

> Hamlet did not place enough value on straightforward, practical deeds, allowing himself instead to lapse into moods of doubt and melancholy.

Hamlet did not place enough value on straight-forward, practical deeds. Instead, he allowed himself to lapse into moods of doubt and melancholy.

These chapters reveal only the surface of her character, its deeper aspects not being revealed until we see her at home with her family.

These chapters reveal only the surface of her character. Its deeper aspects are not revealed until we see her at home with her family.

Here are four long sentences. In some of them – but not all – the writer has run together, into one sentence, what should have been expressed in two. Will you decide which these badly written passages are, and rewrite them in the form of two sentences:

The universe contains millions of stars which are capable of supporting planetary systems, but they lie at vast distances from the earth and it would take some hundreds of light-years to reach them.

One of the great advantages of hang-gliding is that it is a wonderfully silent sport, and as you float over the countryside the only sound is the rush of air past the wings.

Gradually we hauled ourselves up the side of the cliff, digging our toes deep into the crevices and clutching hold of the strongest tufts of grass within reach.

William Golding is one of the most distinguished novelists of recent times, his best known work being *Lord of the Flies*, but he has written a number of other equally original novels.

3 Short and long together

Good writers continually vary the length of their sentences. As a matter of course they avoid writing too many long ones, or too many short ones, one after the other.

Sometimes – to obtain extra force, by making the contrast as sharp as possible – a writer will put a very short sentence after a series of long ones. Here is a passage written by Somerset Maugham. It comes from his essay on Henry Fielding:

> There are some people who cannot read *Tom Jones*. I am not thinking of those who never read anything but the newspapers and the illustrated weeklies, or of those who never read anything but detective stories; I am thinking of those who would not demur if you classed them as members of the intelligentsia, of those who read and re-read *Pride and Prejudice* with delight, *Middlemarch* with self-complacency, and *The Golden Bowl* with reverence. The chances are that it has never occurred to them to read *Tom Jones*; but, sometimes, they have tried and not been able to get on with it. It bores them.

That is splendid writing. There is continual variety. The last sentence in particular, by tightening the rhythm, gives the whole passage an air of alertness and vigour. Here is another example, from the same essay:

> Fielding's enemies accused him of being a political hireling. He was.

Again, by means of a simple contrast between long and short, a little sentence has been loaded with emphasis.

The effect will be the opposite if long sentences are written one after the other, without the relief of shorter ones. Then there will be no sense of rhythm, no rise and fall of emphasis. Slackness will prevail, and the reader will find it heavy going.

Will you now rewrite each of the following passages in the form of two sentences, and in such a way that a short sentence is contrasted with a longer one. In most of the passages – but not in all – the short sentence comes second:

All through the following term, for two hours a week, Paul was made to study Latin, which he hated.

It was a grey November morning, and a thin rain was blowing in from the sea, and huge waves were pounding the rocks off Tregenny Point.

For the layman this is probably the best account of the technique of space travel that has yet been written, being both clear and concise.

When he returned home he saw at once, to his great distress, that a change had come over his mother and that she looked older and more frail.

At this point two members of the team became convinced that the guide had taken the wrong path and so they turned back, with the intention of following the old route across the south face, but were never seen again.

4 Questions

A paragraph should deal with one main topic only. Its opening sentence, or sentences, should indicate what the topic is to be. A pleasing effect can sometimes be obtained by putting the opening sentence into the form of a question, to which the rest of the paragraph is the answer.

> The next point that we will consider is whether we put people in prison to reform them or to punish them.

That sentence (the opening one of a paragraph) does its job. But its tone is forbiddingly heavy.

> Do we put people in prison to reform them or to punish them?

In this form it is lighter and clearer. Instead of dragging the style down, it enlivens it.

Questions sound well, too, when introduced during the course of an argument. In a neat, concise way they make its logic plain: *Why? . . . But is this true? . . . How did he do it?*

Here are some heavily worded paragraph-openings. Will you lighten them by re-phrasing them in the form of questions. The number of words to which each one can be reduced is given in brackets:

> I will begin this essay by trying to find the answer to the question of what the purpose of art is.   (6)

> The question of whether or not there are any advantages in being an only child is the next matter that must occupy our attention.   (9)

We will now consider what the reason is that this kind of music has suddenly become so popular. (10)

We will now enquire into the cause of Hamlet's hesitation. (4)

Let us now consider the matter of how these changes will affect people's lives. (7)

5 Dead words

Very, quite, extremely, completely, utterly, rather, really, absolutely, definitely – there is nothing wrong with these words, but there is something wrong with throwing in one or other of them with almost every adjective or adverb you use. For some students a statement is never *true*, but always *very true*. For them Chaucer's Summoner is never *a wicked man*, but always *a rather wicked man*, or *a really wicked man*. For them so-and-so is never *astonished*, but always *absolutely astonished*. *Definitely* leaves an odd impression of childish triumph: *Macbeth definitely had a conscience.* ('There! I've made up my mind about *that*.') You should think carefully before using this word, since it nearly always weakens rather than strengthens the meaning.

These qualifying words should be handled with caution. The writer who qualifies nearly every statement he makes, emptily and thoughtlessly, is littering his writing with dead words – words that blunt his meaning instead of sharpening it.

Will you now rewrite these sentences exactly as they stand but leaving out any unnecessary words. The number of words needed is given in brackets. As you finish rewriting each sentence compare your version with the longer one and decide which you think is better:

His courage really was absolutely magnificent.   (4)

It was definitely a somewhat frightening experience.
(5)

The overcoming of a disability very often strengthens a person's character quite considerably.   (10)

This is definitely one of Hardy's very best poems. (7)

Gliding really is a most fascinating sport.   (5)

These changes, which were forced through by a group of very incompetent bureaucrats, have completely and utterly destroyed the village.   (16)

6 Dead expressions

It is interesting to note that. . . . – this remark kills all interest. *It is safe to say that. . . .* – perhaps the writer could have taken a risk, and just said it? *It would not be an exaggeration to say that. . . . It is worthy of note that. . . . There is no doubt that. . . . There is reason to believe that* (but the reason is never revealed) *. . . . It is worth pointing out that. . . .* – laboured remarks of this kind are often nothing more than padding.

In some respects. . . . From certain points of view. . . . In some ways. . . . In a way. . . . Somehow. . . . On the whole. . . . – all these expressions are empty of meaning unless the writer goes on to explain *what* respects he has in mind, or *what* points of view, or *what* ways, or why he has qualified his statement by putting *on the whole* in front of it.

Tends to. . . . Has a tendency to. . . . Helps to. . . . Seems to. . . . Serves to. . . . are often used emptily.

This speech tends to deepen our sympathy for him. (This speech deepens. . . .)

This conversation helps to emphasize the difference between Brutus and Cassius. (This conversation emphasizes. . . .)

This incident seems to heighten the tension. (This incident heightens. . . .)

This speech serves to emphasize Duncan's kindness. (This speech emphasizes. . . .)

So, too, are *succeeds in* and *manages to*.

19

The poet succeeds in creating a colourful picture. (The poet creates. . . .)

Chaucer manages to convey a clear impression of the Monk's hypocrisy. (Chaucer conveys. . . .)

Expressions like that last one have a faintly patronizing tone ('Well done, Chaucer').

Now rewrite these sentences, leaving out the unnecessary words:

I must state in the most forthright terms that I definitely disagree with this view. (2)

The characters in this book certainly do tend to come vividly to life. (9)

It must be said that Orwell's satire really is absolutely deadly. (4)

It would not be an exaggeration to say that it was a rather lonely job. (5)

It is safe to say that the most important requirement of a novel is that it should have a really good story to it. (15)

I will begin by pointing out that there is absolutely no truth whatever in this statement. (7)

7 'Also'

Also often sounds ugly when placed at the beginning of a sentence:

Also he could play the trumpet.

Taken into the flow of the sentence, it sounds much better:

He could also play the trumpet.

Also this speech reveals a certain weakness in Juliet's character.

This speech also reveals a certain weakness in Juliet's character.

Also he was the strongest boy in the group.

He was also the strongest boy in the group.

In these sentences *also* is used lightly, without emphasis, in the sense of 'in addition', or 'as well'. Sometimes more stress is laid on it. Standing awkwardly at the head of a sentence, often with a comma after it, it is made to do duty as *moreover* – that is to say, it is used to show that a new line of thought, or a new idea, is being introduced:

Also, they never expected that this threat would be taken seriously.

Also, as soon as we began to consider this route we found that certain parts of it had never been properly mapped out.

Also, however hard they tried to disguise the fact, many of the poets of that generation were more interested in politics than art.

In contexts like these it is nearly always better to use *moreover*. Try re-reading those three sentences with *moreover* as the first word, and you will notice the improvement.

Now improve each of the following sentences by moving the *also* forward:

Also this film has been shown in France and America.

Also she gave him her father's gold watch.

Also mountaineering can be a very humbling experience.

Also Surrey is a very beautiful county.

Also these rare birds can be seen occasionally in the north of Scotland.

8 *Incomplete sentences*

Occasionally, in order to achieve some particular effect, a writer may leave a sentence, or a series of sentences, incomplete:

> A grey, wet day. A high wind ruffling the poplars. Rain flowing like a waterfall over the pavilion roof.

There, the aim is to suggest that the writer is making a swift sketch of the scene, in a few brisk strokes.

> Been alarmed, have you, by this latest trend? Not to worry. Not unduly, anyway. Because here are the facts. . . .

The writer of that newspaper item wants us to feel that we are listening to a matey sort of bloke who is just chatting to us in his natural manner.

There is no harm in writing incomplete sentences if you have some special reason for doing so. But it is quite a different matter if you leave them incomplete not deliberately, in order to gain an effect, but through carelessness:

> Today the world seems a very small place. A good bit smaller, in fact, than a single country would have seemed fifty years ago. Business men travelling to distant capitals as a matter of routine. Television linking together people who live thousands of miles apart. Quite different from earlier times.

That writer simply followed the disjointed patterns of casual, everyday chat; and he did so because that was what came most easily to him. He had no particular purpose in mind. Incomplete sentences of that kind spoil written English. They make it seem slapdash and poorly conceived.

Will you now rewrite that last passage (about the world seeming small) in such a way that all the sentences are complete. Re-shape it and re-word it in any way you like, but do not alter the meaning.

9 Tenses

Never switch about from one tense to another. To do so is sheer carelessness. Here are some examples of this very irritating mistake:

It was a cold December night. It is snowing hard, but the sitting-room, where we are having our coffee, was warm and comfortable.

Outside, it was much darker than we expected it to be, because the wind has swept a bank of cloud across the sky, obscuring the moon and the stars.

We moved forward at a steady pace. On either side of us the trees rustled, making us wonder if ghosts are lurking there.

The Wife of Bath is heavily over-dressed. She wore a huge hat, bright red stockings, and new shoes.

Iago persuades Roderigo to go to Cyprus even before he has decided exactly what use he was going to make of him.

Will you now rewrite those passages in such a way as to eliminate the inconsistencies in the use of tenses. In the three narrative passages it will be best to keep to the past tense. But in the two about literature the present tense will probably be more suitable. When writing answers to literature questions you will often find it convenient to use the present. Chaucer is dead; but he is not dead as a writer – so we can write: 'Chaucer brings this character vividly to life.' Hamlet lived long ago; but fictitious characters do not die – so we can write: 'Hamlet is tormented by doubts.'

10 'So' and 'such'

Never use *so* or *such* purely to emphasize a straightforward statement.

The meeting was so interesting.

He was so disappointed.

She laughed in such a sweet way.

It was such a surprise to him.

The music was so beautiful.

All those sentences sound silly and sentimental because *so* and *such* have been wrongly used. Whenever one or other of these words is used in this sort of context the sentence must be continued into a second clause introduced by the word *that*. In those sentences, therefore, we must either leave out the *so*'s and the *such*'s or else we must write:

The meeting was so interesting that I was sorry when it came to an end.

He was so disappointed that he leant on my shoulder and wept.

She laughed in such a sweet way that everyone turned to look at her.

It was such a surprise to him that he nearly fainted.

The music was so beautiful that it made me catch my breath.

Notice, however, that sometimes, when they occur in subordinate clauses, *so* and *such* can be used as emphasizing

26

words without producing a bad effect:

All the delegates were young. That is why the meeting was such a triumphant success.

A person who is so careless, over such a simple matter, cannot be trusted.

In three of the following sentences the *so* or the *such* should not be there. Will you write those three sentences out, leaving out the unwanted words:

The ending of the play was so sad that I could hardly bear to watch it.

She liked living there because it was such a lonely place.

He had such a wonderful gift for understanding people.

The weather was so perfect.

We had not realized that he could be so obstinate.

A holiday by the sea is so much more exciting when there are opportunities for surfing and yachting.

11 'Is when'

In most contexts *is when* does not make sense.

> A good view of the lake is when you reach the top of the path.

We cannot write 'when you reach' unless something happens in the first part of the sentence, and in that case nothing does. So we will *make* something happen, and then the *when* will have something to attach itself to:

> You *get* a good view of the lake when you reach the top of the path.

Here is another example:

> The climax of the film is when Joe is murdered.

This time it will be more convenient to leave the first part of the sentence unaltered, and have nothing happen, and get rid of the *when*:

> The climax of the film is the murder of Joe.

Here are some more examples:

> The Council's worst mistake was when they allowed these flats to be built.

> The Council made their worst mistake when they allowed these flats to be built.

Or:

> The Council's worst mistake was to allow these flats to be built.

A good example of Chaucer's sly humour is when he describes the Nun's table manners.

Chaucer's description of the Nun's table manners is a good example of his sly humour.

The most dramatic scene is in the churchyard when the convict confronts Pip.

The most dramatic scene is the one in which the convict confronts Pip in the churchyard.

A further simile is when Tennyson likens the mountain stream to a 'downward smoke'.

In a further simile Tennyson likens the mountain stream to a 'downward smoke'.

Such expressions as *the scene where, the scene when, the chapter where*, are also unpleasantly inaccurate.

The scene where Duncan and Banquo arrive. . . .

The scene in which Duncan and Banquo arrive. . . .

The chapter where Wells describes Mr Polly's education. . . .

The chapter in which Wells describes Mr Polly's education. . . .

Now re-shape these sentences:

The most unexpected event in the film is when the hidden documents are discovered.

One of the worst disasters of that decade was when the *Titanic* sank.

A big surprise was when we turned the corner and saw that the road was blocked.

The deepest kind of silence is when it comes suddenly and unexpectedly.

A simile is when you liken one thing to another.

Caesar's last words are when he says 'Et tu, Brute?'

Brutus's great blunder was when he decided to allow Antony to address the citizens.

12 'This', 'which' and 'showing'

His most recent novel was hailed by one critic as a minor classic. This pleased him enormously.

When we read that sentence we understand at once what the *this* refers back to. But people sometimes use a *this* at the beginning of a sentence when what it refers back to is not clear at all:

As we approached the house we could see at a glance that certain parts of it were badly in need of repair – especially the beautiful mansard roof which the agent had praised so highly. This was a great disappointment to us.

For a moment the reader is misled into thinking that it was the roof which was the disappointment – which of course it was; but that is not what the writer meant.

Which is sometimes used in the same misleading way:

If you take this road into Oxford you get many glimpses, from far off, of its beautiful clusters of spires and of Magdalen's sturdy tower, which makes you eager to reach the city and explore it.

Is it Magdalen's tower that makes you eager? Is that what the writer meant?

Finally, the word *showing* is sometimes used loosely too – that is, in such a way that it is not clearly related to what the writer intended it to refer to:

The protest against the threatened closure of the

31

theatre was so widely supported that the Council finally agreed to allow it to remain open, showing how popular this repertory company has become in our town.

It is true that the Council's change of heart did show, indirectly, how popular the company had become, but that is not what the writer meant.

Will you now look back to the first muddled piece of writing we considered – about the house in need of repair – and rewrite the second sentence in such a way as to get rid of the misleading *this*.

Next, look at the second passage, about Oxford. Assume that you are writing it and that you have got as far as putting the comma after 'tower'. Now complete the rest of it in such a way as to get rid of the muddle caused by the *which*.

Now rewrite the last part of the last passage, about the closure of the theatre. Again, assume that you are writing it and that you have got as far as 'open', but instead of a comma you have put a full stop there. Now complete it. How are you going to begin that last sentence? Ask yourself, 'Exactly what was it that showed how popular the repertory company had become?'

13 Pronouns

Pronouns give a splendid effect of clarity and economy. You should use them whenever you can. Use them even when there may seem to be a risk of confusion. For they have a much stronger tendency to attach themselves to the right nouns than many people realize. A reader is not going to insist, perversely, on attaching them to the wrong ones, against the sense of a passage, just in order to make nonsense of it.

Here, now, are seven passages. Will you rewrite the second sentence of each one in such a way that you do not repeat *any* of the nouns mentioned in the first sentence, but use pronouns instead. As you complete the rewriting of each one, read over what you have written and notice how much more fluent the English sounds when the pronouns are used:

John was terrified of Mr Bates. Yet John bravely confronted Mr Bates and ordered Mr Bates to leave.

My favourite painter is David Hockney. David Hockney's best pictures, in my opinion, are fine works of art.

Anne's attempts to persuade her father that the programme was harmless were of no avail. Anne's father would not let Anne watch the programme.

Carol decided that a pearl brooch would set off her black dress perfectly. So Carol went out that afternoon and bought a pearl brooch.

There have been many explanations of the origin of human life. The oldest explanation is that God created human life.

Chaucer describes the Pardoner in a tone of sneering contempt. We are left in no doubt that Chaucer despises the Pardoner.

Soon after leaving Juliet, Romeo approaches Friar Laurence. Romeo tells Friar Laurence of his love for Juliet and asks for Friar Laurence's help.

14 Doubling conjunctions

A word like *which* can be used twice in the same sentence in order to introduce two parallel clauses:

> These documents, which he carried in a brief-case, and which he claimed were genuine, were in fact a bundle of forgeries.

There is nothing wrong in using *which* twice in that way. But if we use it twice in such a way as to make the second clause it introduces dependent on the first one, we shall produce a clumsy sentence:

> These documents, which he carried in a brief-case, which he kept locked, were in fact. . . .

What is true of *which* is true of other conjunctions too. The following sentences are all clumsy because in each one the conjunction is doubled:

> We were disappointed when we revisited this part of the coast because it had been completely spoilt because a big caravan site had been put there.

> When you visit poor countries you begin to think how fortunate you are when you see children begging for food.

> Some people think that space travel is a waste of money. But this great adventure cannot be measured in terms of money alone, but perhaps too much is spent on it.

Will you now improve those three passages. Re-shape them as much as you like, but do not alter the meaning.

15 Prepositions

Prepositions are sometimes used in a way which is unpleasantly inaccurate, as in the following examples. The correction is given in brackets.

This scene makes a sharp contrast from the previous one (with).

The underlying theme in his speech . . . (of).

The poem has a regular rhythm to it. (The poem has a regular rhythm.)

There was a lack of understanding by the men (on the part of).

They gathered by the untidiness of the kitchen that she had left in a hurry (from).

With the Summoner Chaucer's attitude is quite different. (Chaucer's attitude towards the Summoner is quite different.)

Chaucer adopts a different method with the Friar (when describing).

The scenes with Laertes . . . (in which Laertes appears).

Lear expresses his feelings with words that summon up vague suggestions of time and vastness (in).

Iago replied, with a tone of bitter contempt, that he would never speak another word (in).

Now improve these sentences:

She had a wide knowledge on these matters.

By what we heard we could only conclude that he had left home.

We were unable to obtain any information on this.

They had left no clue of where they had gone.

Juliet expresses her grief with words that are deeply poetical.

The scene with Banquo murdered is one of the best in the play.

16 Tautology

Tautology is the useless repetition of the same idea in different words. Two words of similar meaning are used when one would have done:

The heartbreak and the despair.

Compassion and pity.

She hated and resented him.

Shrewd and perceptive.

Troubled and anxious.

A wicked villain.

A sudden shock.

A perfect ideal.

Sometimes two phrases, or two sentences, are used:

The tale never becomes monotonous: it is always varied and interesting.

She had a dependable husband – someone she could rely on.

The author keeps to the point and does not wander off into irrelevancies.

He was the prop of her world: without him her world would have collapsed.

The doubt may occasionally arise: is this or that expression a piece of tautology or is it a proper use of two

distinct words? A simple test is to ask: could we put *both...
and also* in front of the words? What about *conflict and
strife*? *Both conflict and also strife* is obviously repetitive. What
about *sad and tragic*? Could we write *both sad and also tragic*?
Perhaps there is a distinction. But, if there is, it is a subtle
one, and we are under an obligation to the reader to
explain it to him. If we pass it by without referring to it he
will rightly conclude that the words are a piece of useless
repetition.

Some students have a way of refusing to own up to
tautology. Of course no two words have exactly the same
meaning, and a writer can easily convince himself after-
wards that he used two words instead of one because he was
anxious to convey some subtle shade of difference – when in
fact he never gave the matter a thought.

Tautology can also take the form of simple repetition:
exactly the same point is made twice. The duplication is
irritating to the reader:

Throughout the whole chapter. . . .

But after a while, however, he began to realize. . . .

That is how it first began.

At about two o'clock or thereabouts.

Then after that. . . .

The final incident with which the chapter ends. . . .

The experiences they shared together. . . .

These factors combined together to produce. . . .

Apparently he seemed to be unaware. . . .

He will have to try yet harder still.

This was also part of his purpose too.

He could do no more than just follow blindly.

The daily papers that regularly appear. . . .

Now look at these sentences. Six of them contain some form of duplication. Will you rewrite those six in such a way as to eliminate it:

He made the same journey every Tuesday, at exactly the same time.

Inevitably, under these circumstances, he was bound to fail.

At half past six exactly the first batch of evening papers appeared on the streets.

It was nothing more than just a passing phase.

He left home exactly one year ago to the day.

With every year that passed he became more and more embittered.

He showed that he was equally as capable of a sustained effort as any other member of the team.

This alteration made the play even better still.

After a while the moon reappeared again.

17 Slang

> The author of this excellent book has made a lifetime's study of film history, and the knowledge he has accumulated is tempered by a fine sense of judgement. He devotes a whole chapter to an analysis of horror films. These films, in his view, do much more than just frighten the pants off us: they enable us to indulge our fantasies and exorcise our fears.

Using a slang expression in that way is fine. The vigour it injects into the writing derives from the contrast, from the fact that it crops up unexpectedly, amidst a flow of cultured English.

> The author has put a terrific lot into this book and he comes up with some pretty good ideas. There's a lot of stuff on horror films and how they don't just frighten the pants off you but also help you get rid of your hang-ups.

Writing of that kind has no vigour at all. It is the writing of someone who uses slang expressions not just occasionally, as a contrast, but all the time, because they are the first words that come to his mind and using them saves him the trouble of looking any further.

To use slang effectively a writer needs to have at his command a range of language, for the effectiveness depends on contrast – on his being able to place, in a context of accomplished fluency, just the right piece of throw-away chat.

18 Choosing the specific adjective or adverb

Good, bad, badly, brilliant, marvellous, dreadfully, terribly – generalized adjectives and adverbs of this kind are sometimes useful. But more often than not you will find that you can improve your style by being more specific. Try to find the word that will tell the reader not merely that something is *good*, but in what way it is good.

> This is a good portrait . . . a clear portrait? . . . a realistic portrait? . . . a convincing portrait? . . . a life-like portrait? . . . a detailed portrait? . . . an amusing portrait?

> This is a good metaphor . . . an inspired metaphor? . . . a colourful metaphor? . . . a concise metaphor? . . . an original metaphor?

> This is a bad metaphor . . . an unconvincing metaphor? . . . a colourless metaphor? . . . an awkward metaphor? . . . a far-fetched metaphor? . . . a trite metaphor?

> She was a terrible hypocrite . . . a confirmed hypocrite? . . . a shameless hypocrite? . . . a plausible hypocrite?

If you are making a general statement you may find that you can still do better than choose words like *good* or *bad*:

> This is a good simile because. . . . This is an effective simile because. . . .

> What makes this description so good . . . so vivid. . . .

What makes this description so bad . . . so flat. . . .

It may be helpful, sometimes, when choosing an adjective or an adverb, to think of a scale. One end of it is the general end, the other the specific end. Always try to move as far as you can towards the specific end. Often you will find that you can move a long way: *very satisfying*, for example, can be changed to *deeply satisfying; very experienced* to *widely experienced; very overloaded* to *heavily overloaded; brilliant insight* to *sharp insight*, or *shrewd insight; a great dislike* to *a strong dislike*, or *a bitter dislike* – and so on.

Some generalized adverbial expressions, in certain contexts, sound embarrassingly naive:

Hamlet loved Ophelia very much. (Hamlet loved Ophelia deeply.)

Now suggest a more precise adjective or adverb for each of the following expressions or sentences. Choose a different one each time:

A good musician. . . . He had a good brain. . . . It was not a very good explanation.

A bad argument. . . . A bad decision. . . . The discipline was very bad. . . . A bad mistake.

A marvellous actor. . . . An awful speech. . . . These horrible hoardings ruin the view. . . . A big risk. . . . A big handicap.

The streets were terribly hot. . . . The sun was terribly bright. . . . He was terrifically intelligent. . . . We were terrifically impressed by his bravery.

19 Choosing the simple word

Some students, as soon as they take up a pen, seem to find it difficult to think of the ordinary, clear words of the language. Instead of *try* they write *endeavour*; instead of *show, demonstrate*; instead of *tell, inform*; instead of *too, excessively*; instead of *long, lengthy*; instead of *begin, commence*; instead of *most of the time, the majority of the time*; instead of *buy, purchase*; instead of *enough, sufficient*; instead of *because, on account of the fact that*; instead of *many, numerous*; instead of *often, on numerous occasions* . . . and so on. They write in this way because they feel that in order to write well they must adopt a learned tone, and choose words that sound impressive. In fact, that is the way to write badly. For a writer's aim should be to convey his meaning as clearly as he can. If, instead, he aims at creating an impression, he will make his meaning less clear, and at the same time sound pompous and foolish.

So never choose the word that is more complicated, or more literary, or more learned, just because you think it sounds impressive. The words that sound truly impressive are the simple ones.

Will you now suggest a simpler word that could replace the more elaborate one that has been used in each of these sentences:

> He exhibited a great deal of courage. . . . We did not anticipate that they would arrive so soon. . . . The village we reside in. . . . They did not need our

assistance. . . . She committed one serious mistake. . . .
They are going to construct six houses on this site. . . .
The envelope was concealed under a cushion. . . . For
the greater proportion of the time. . . . There were
approximately forty people in the room. . . . He
concluded his speech with an appeal for money.

20 Avoiding the undignified word

A simple style has dignity. A casual style, made up of conversational mannerisms and expressions, has none. In literature answers, especially, slang expressions are liable to cause a collapse into absurdity:

It is difficult to understand what makes Caliban tick.

Then King Lear simply blew up.

In the meanwhile Othello had worked himself up into a really dreadful state.

Even the Queen did not realize that Hamlet was kidding.

Expressions like these are glaringly wrong; but there are many others that are bad in a less obvious way:

The poet puts over the sadness of the scene. (conveys)

Ophelia was scared. (frightened)

Maybe Caliban was right. (Perhaps)

In this scene Macbeth shows quite a bit of feeling. (some feeling)

The pathos of the scene comes over to the reader. (is felt by the reader)

There are quite a few sad moments in this story. (some sad moments)

The poet then brings in a simile. (introduces)

This detail adds a bit of realism to the scene. (a touch of realism)

Keats next talks about the different pictures on the urn. (describes)

In this verse there is a cunning suggestion that . . . (subtle)

A strange sadness hangs around this story. (haunts)

In this scene Macbeth's conscience is bothering him. (troubling)

Then Antony brings up the subject of Caesar's will. (introduces)

Then Cassius brings up another argument. (puts forward)

In this scene another side of Hamlet's character comes out. (is revealed)

Iago found it easy to fool Othello about the hand-kerchief. (deceive)

After a bit. . . . (After a while. . . . After a few moments. . . .)

Pretty well all the time. . . . (Nearly all the time. . . .)

She had lots more courage than her husband. (far more)

A whole lot of these ideas. . . . (Many of)

This joke always causes lots of laughter. (a great deal of laughter)

We hear an awful lot of bad music today. (a great deal of bad music)

One might just as well make out that it is wrong to keep cows for their milk. (argue . . . maintain)

As soon as his wife has left, Macbeth begins talking to himself. (begins a soliloquy . . . begins to soliloquize)

The world is in an awful mess. (in a troubled state . . . in a chaotic state . . . in a state of conflict and confusion)

Antony then puts on an act of being overcome with grief. (pretends to be)

As far as beauty of form is concerned, the ode 'To Autumn' beats all the other odes. (surpasses)

In this scene an argument starts up between Cassius and Brutus. (begins . . . develops)

Iago keeps on about the handkerchief. (keeps mentioning)

The poet then switches back to his opening theme. (returns)

The poet makes up a vivid picture. (creates)

They were afraid that his speech would start something up. (cause trouble)

Then Hamlet comes on. (appears . . . enters)

After Hamlet has gone off. . . . (left)

Hamlet's next move. . . . (step)

The poet harps on the idea that life is futile. (dwells)

He had one final go at regaining his self-composure. (He made one final attempt to regain his self-composure.)

Here are some more sentences that lack dignity. Will you rewrite them and improve the style:

This unfortunate incident mucked up our holiday.

Some of the more violent scenes on the television turn me up.

One remark he made really stuck in my mind.

Many years ago, before cars had been thought up. . . .

What got me most about this film was the wonderful photography of the mountain scenery.

Claudius thought he could kid Hamlet.

Antony wound up his speech with a moving appeal to the citizens' sense of pity.

21 'Thing'

Thing is a word that often sounds slovenly. Try to replace it with the name of whatever 'thing' it is:

The most dramatic thing in the play. . . . (event . . . incident)

One thing about this writer's style. . . . (One feature of this writer's style. . . .)

All kinds of interesting things are shown on the television. (programmes)

One thing that occurred during the journey upset her deeply. (incident)

The most tragic thing about Ophelia's death. . . . (The most tragic aspect of Ophelia's death. . . .)

In this scene another thing in Hamlet's character is revealed. (another aspect of Hamlet's character. . . . another side of Hamlet's character. . . .)

Iago knows that Othello will imagine all kinds of things. (possibilities)

Stephen's soul was deeply wounded by this kind of thing. (treatment)

Many old people find it difficult to keep in touch with things. (life)

The things he said about his cousin. . . . (The remarks he made)

These things suggest that the Nun paid too much attention to her appearance. (These details)

Things like this give the play a deep sadness. (Touches like this)

This metaphor suggests two things. (two ideas)

The thing that was uppermost in his mind. . . . (The thought)

Will you now rewrite these sentences. In each one, replace *thing* with a more precise word:

To be caught up in this kind of violence is a very frightening thing.

Some of the things he put forward in his speech. . . .

The loss of the R101, in 1930, was one of the worst things in the history of aviation.

The most popular thing in the programme. . . .

In my opinion the preservation of wild life is a thing that is well worth striving for.

The conquest of Mount Everest was a truly heroic thing.

22 'Just' and 'simply'

There is a colloquial use of *just*, before adjectives and verbs, which should always be avoided in writing:

The audience just loved his singing.

He was just determined to marry her.

When he first appears on the stage Edmund is just full of resentment.

The delay seemed just endless.

In those sentences *just* has been used, not in one of its proper senses, but as a means of emphasizing the word that follows it. If ever you find that you have used it in this way you should cross it out.

Simply, too, is sometimes used in the same way:

The damage was simply enormous.

His generosity was simply wonderful.

Everyone who knew her simply adored her.

In each of those sentences it should be crossed out, since it has been used not in its proper sense, but as a means of emphasis, in a way that is colloquial and childish.

Here are some more sentences in which *just* and *simply* are used. In three of them they are used in a weak sense. Will you write out those three, leaving out the *just* or the *simply*:

They were only just in time.

The front of the building was simply proportioned.

He was just over six foot tall.

The view was simply magnificent.

The film lasted just one hour and six minutes.

She just wanted to be left in peace.

She just longed to get married and have children of her own.

He just never arrived on time.

23 'Says', 'calls' and 'gets'

Says, in some contexts, is too colloquial:

> Chaucer says that the Squire is about twenty years of age.

We could write *Chaucer states* instead, or *Chaucer writes*, but both these expressions sound stilted; so we will write:

> Chaucer tells us that the Squire is about twenty years of age.

Here are some more examples:

> As he enters the courtyard Banquo says that the stars are completely hidden (remarks).

> Antony then says that he has no intention of contradicting Brutus (declares).

> Cassius, who was more cautious, said that it would be wiser to delay the attack (argued, maintained).

> Ophelia is heartbroken, and at the end of her speech she says 'O woe is me!' (cries out).

Calls, too, sometimes sounds wrong:

> Chaucer calls the Squire a 'lover and a lusty bachelor'.

> Chaucer describes the Squire as a 'lover and a lusty bachelor'.

> John of Gaunt calls England a 'precious stone set in the silver sea'.

John of Gaunt compares England to a 'precious stone set in the silver sea'.

Gets and *got* are sometimes undignified:

As soon as Banquo gets to the palace gates. . . . (reaches).

This poem has got several metaphors (has).

He got a good reputation in the wars against the heathens (won).

The poet gets this effect by including several unusual adjectives (achieves).

Will you now improve these sentences:

This book has recently got very popular.

After a short delay the train got moving again.

We got to our destination sooner than we expected.

The scenery in this part of the county has got more variety to it.

Only a few moments before he is stabbed Caesar says he is unassailable.

Romeo calls the window at which Juliet appears 'the east' and he says that Juliet herself is 'the sun'.

24 'Add to', 'increase' and 'lessen'

Students sometimes use these verbs loosely, without troubling to find a more exact verb:

This line adds to the poetic effect (heightens).

This scene adds to the tension (heightens).

These details add to the picture (enhance, enrich).

This speech increases the atmosphere of wildness and terror (intensifies).

This aspect of Brutus's character increases the contrast between him and Cassius (sharpens).

This digression lessens the monotony (relieves).

There was not a trace of sunlight to lessen the gloom (relieve, lighten).

This line lessens the effect of the poem as a whole (weakens).

It is not suggested that 'add to', 'increase' or 'lessen' are necessarily wrong, or even bad, in all the above examples – merely that the style is improved, in each case, if the word given in brackets is used instead.

Will you now improve the following sentences in the same way:

These touches add to the sadness of the play.

These details increase the realism of the scene.

This knowledge increased our awareness of the dangers we were facing.

As the hours went by the gloom increased.

The inclusion of a harp in the orchestra greatly adds to this piece of music.

This disappointment lessened his enthusiasm.

The slight pause he made added to the impact of his reply.

25 Abstract expressions

Always express your ideas in as direct a manner as possible. Some people have a way of introducing abstract nouns into their writing quite unnecessarily, with the result that what could have been a perfectly straightforward statement becomes obscure:

> The occurrence of the mistake was due to our inability to read his writing.

In other words:

> The mistake occurred because we could not read his writing.

> The reason for her despising her husband was that he was lazy.

> She despised her husband because he was lazy.

> The other children picked on her because of her smallness and timidity.

> The other children picked on her because she was small and timid.

> This setback brought about a strengthening of his determination.

> This setback strengthened his determination.

> There is a great deal of irregularity in the metre.

> The metre is very irregular.

> There is a complete absence of imagery in this poem.

There is no imagery in this poem.

Caesar had an acute awareness of this flaw in his character.

Caesar was acutely aware of this flaw in his character.

Chaucer has admiration for the Knight.

Chaucer admires the Knight.

There is also a mention by Chaucer of the Monk's love of hunting.

Chaucer also mentions the Monk's love of hunting.

Now re-shape these sentences in such a way that the meaning is expressed in a direct manner:

He was dismissed because of his refusal to obey the rules.

The beauty of the view was so great that we did not want to leave.

It will take three more days to achieve the completion of the task.

These changes will bring about a great improvement in the play.

The steepness of the slope was such that we were able to move forward only very slowly.

26 Active and passive

The active form of the verb is clear and direct. You should never twist it into the passive when there is no need to.

> In earlier times a much more important part was played in people's lives by religion.

> In earlier times religion played a much more important part in people's lives.

> The main block is led up to by a long drive, lined with trees.

> A long drive, lined with trees, leads up to the main block.

> In this chapter a very clear idea is conveyed by William Golding of the meaning behind the story.

> In this chapter William Golding conveys a very clear idea of the meaning behind the story.

> Roderigo's infatuation with Desdemona is made use of by Iago.

> Iago makes use of Roderigo's infatuation with Desdemona.

In all those examples the passive form is bad because it is not really a passive at all, but an active form clumsily twisted round. There is nothing wrong with a true passive:

> They found him lying near a ditch: he had been knocked down and robbed.

The passive forms which occur in the following sentences

are all clumsy and unnecessary. Will you rewrite the sentences and change these forms into the active:

In his speech this point was very clearly explained by him.

A firm of architects have now bought the house, and an undertaking has been given by them not to alter it in any way.

A touch of humour is added to the film by the sudden appearance of this eccentric character.

This scene is brought vividly to life by Lawrence.

The longings of a downtrodden people are expressed by this song.

The witches are first encountered by Macbeth when he is making his way across the heath with Banquo.

27 Full stops and commas

Two mistakes are always being made. They are made so often that they could be described as the two curses of students' writing. One is putting a comma, instead of a full stop, at the end of a sentence that is grammatically complete:

> Cambridge is a beautiful city, its most impressive features are its wide quadrangles and the quiet meadows that form a background to them.

A comma should never be used, as it has been in that passage, to separate one sentence from another. In that case, as it happens, the reader is not muddled by the mistake. But that was pure luck – because he very often will be:

> It is unlikely that this stretch of meadowland will ever be spoilt, because it contains such a wonderful variety of wild life, and also perhaps because they respect its beauty, the College Governors have made an order that it must never be built on.

The other mistake is using only one comma when two are needed. Two commas are often used to enclose a group of words and set them aside from the rest of the sentence. They work in partnership, as a pair:

> There is a tradition, dating back to medieval times, that the waters of this lake have healing properties.

In that sentence we pause for both the commas; so neither of them is likely to get missed out. But very often we do not pause at all for the first one of the pair:

It would be easy, I think, to lose your way on these moors.

This, then, is the conclusion I have reached.

By the end of the week, however, the situation had changed.

In sentences like those we must be especially careful to put in the first of the two commas, because the voice passes over it so quickly that it is easy to forget it.

In the following passage the ends of some of the sentences have been marked by commas instead of full stops. Will you write it out and put these mistakes right:

These two old people lived on their own, and often they felt lonely. For many years their son, who was their only child, had lived with them, now he had grown up and left home, and they hardly ever saw him. Their house was very isolated, their nearest neighbours lived nearly a mile away, and so their only companions were the birds and animals in the woods. But on this particular evening they did not feel lonely, they had a guest, their nephew, Derek, whom they had known since he had been a child, was staying with them.

In the next passage four commas are missing. Will you write it out, with those commas put in:

Derek had arrived early that afternoon. He had taken a taxi which was the only form of transport, from Littledean Station. The roads were almost snowbound. A blizzard had raged the taxi driver told him, all the previous day. No gritting it seemed, was ever undertaken in those remote country districts, for the surfaces of all the roads particularly at the sides, were corrugated into white trenches.

28 Colons, semi-colons and dashes

A colon marks the end of a sentence, just as a full stop does. But it differs from a full stop in this respect: it tells the reader that in the next sentence there is going to be an explanation of what has just been said. When we are reading aloud and we come to a colon we do not lower the voice fully, as we do for a full stop: we keep it half raised and expectant.

> This route had two serious disadvantages: it was very steep, and in some places the path had crumbled away.

> They soon found out what had caused the derailment: a section of the line had fractured.

> He will not be able to compete tomorrow: he has torn a ligament in his ankle.

> This plan has one great weakness: it makes no allowance for even the smallest error of judgement.

A semi-colon has none of the forward-pointing momentum that a colon has. It is like a weak full stop: it ends a sentence, as a full stop does, but more gently. You should use one when you feel that a full stop would mark your sentence off too sharply from the one that follows:

> It is a dull time of year. The amusement parks are closed for the winter; the promenade is deserted.

> Time works its changes. Great men become famous and then die and are forgotten; empires rise and fall;

wars are fought, and there is suffering and destruction.

Semi-colons should be used sparingly. A write who throws them in freely, when they are not really needed, all through his work, instead of ending his sentences properly with full stops, makes his writing look casual and slapdash.

A dash is a useful punctuation mark. It can be used to direct the reader's attention forward to a single word, or to a short phrase:

She accused him of giving way to the weakness he despised most – cowardice.

His character is like his clothes – dull and shabby.

He had one fatal weakness – a love of flattery.

Commas in these sentences, instead of dashes, would not be right.

A writer may also use a dash if he wants to add an after-thought to something he has just written, or if he wants to make a brief comment on it:

He was very pleased with the decision they reached at last week's committee meeting – or at least he said he was.

They decided to take the path that led across the mountains by the northern pass – a dangerous route.

Tempted in this way, Cassio gets drunk – not helplessly, but enough for Iago's purposes.

Dashes can also be used in pairs to mark off a parenthesis. They mark it off more sharply than commas do, and they should be used when commas would not be sharp enough:

On the contrary – and this is the important point – it

was only because he did not know what he was doing that he succeeded so brilliantly.

If we turn to Hazlitt – and there is no greater critic – we will find a different opinion expressed.

Othello's finest qualities – his courage, his honesty, the aristocratic pride that he never loses – are all revealed.

Finally, a dash can be used to pull a sentence together, usually after a list:

Manly courage, honesty, and kindness of heart – these were the qualities that made Prince Henry so popular among all classes of Englishmen.

Six of the commas are wrong in the next passage: two of them should have been colons, and four of them dashes. Write the passage out with these mistakes put right:

Derek was a town-bred boy, and in his view country life had one great drawback, there was nothing to do in the evenings. The time between supper and bedtime always passed very slowly, so slowly, in fact, that Derek sometimes found himself wishing that he had never come on the visit. On this particular evening, after reading a magazine for a while, he did what he had done on every previous evening that week, he made his excuses to his uncle and aunt and went to bed early.

His bedroom, it was really his uncle's study converted into a bedroom, was on the ground floor, and its window faced directly on to the woods. Derek got into bed and lay there, unable to sleep. After a while he heard a strange sound coming from outside his window, a sort of breathy, whistling sound.

29 *Presenting quotations*

If a quotation is as long as a complete line of poetry, or
longer, separate it from your commentary by starting it on
a new line and setting it in from the margin. Do not use
quotation marks: setting the passage out, in its own space,
does away with the need for them. When you resume your
commentary start a new line again, beginning (unless you
happen to be opening a new paragaph) against the left-
hand margin.

> Macbeth is a good liar:
>> O! yet I do repent me of my fury,
>> That I did kill them.
> But Macduff, who has been watching him closely, is
> already suspicious.

In an examination you will not have time to quote long
speeches, and you will not be expected to. If you want to
indicate that you are referring to the whole of a speech,
quote the opening phrase and put a row of dots after it:

> Othello addresses the Senators quietly and con-
> fidently:
>> Most potent, grave, and reverend signiors. . . .

If you quote two or more passages consecutively, put a
row of dots after each one, to separate them:

> Othello often speaks of his past:
>> I fetch my life and being
>> From men of royal siege. . . .
>> Wherein I spake of most disastrous chances,

> Of moving accidents by flood and field. . . .
>   That handkerchief
> Did an Egyptian to my mother give. . . .

You can use a quotation to complete the sense of your own sentence. Put a dash (*not* a colon) to lead the reader's eye forward:

> Prospero describes how Antonio's ministers prepared –
>   A rotten carcass of a butt, not rigg'd,
>   Nor tackle, sail, nor mast.

> In a mood of happy anticipation Prospero tells Ariel to –
>   bring a corollary
>   Rather than want a spirit.

You can also continue your own sentence into a quotation, and complete it after it. Again, put dashes, to lead the reader through the quotation:

> The contrast between Banquo and Macbeth is made plain at the beginning, when they meet the witches. While the gentle Banquo asks them mildly –
>   Live you? or are you aught
>   That men may question?
> – the more aggressive Macbeth pushes forward and orders them to speak.

If a quotation is only a short one – a single word, perhaps, or a short phrase – introduce it into your own commentary by underlining it or by using quotation marks. (Underlining a word you write produces the equivalent, in print, of italics.)

> Shakespeare has peopled his island with strange creatures. There are apes that 'mow and chatter',

adders with 'cloven tongues', and elves that chase the ebbing tide across the sands 'with printless foot'.

Most quotations from prose works should be short extracts. You will gain nothing by memorizing a long passage, word for word, and setting it out in full in your examination answer. The purpose of including quotations in your answers is to support or illustrate your argument, not to show that you know them by heart.

Lawrence admires the fox. It is a 'lovely dog-fox in its prime'. It has a belly as 'white and soft as snow', a 'wonderful black-glinted brush', and a 'thick splendour of a tail'.

If you introduce a series of short quotations consecutively, separate them by putting dots between them:

Miranda expresses her wonder in simple words: 'a brave form . . . a thing divine . . . he's gentle'.

Simon keeps up a flow of banter: 'I wonder if there's any likelihood of dinner. . . . Now then, sir, there's a bird here waiting for you. . . . Here's something to make your hair curl.'

Brackets are useful:

Stephen remembered the girl's low voice (she 'murmured as if fascinated') and the way the boy staggered into the room under his load of coal.

Uncle Charles's efforts to stop the argument ('come now! . . . it's too bad surely') had no effect.

Othello restrains himself from dwelling on the topic ('No more of that') and turns to the last question that remains to be settled.

Gonzalo did not hear the words of the song that Ariel

sang in his ear ('While you here do snoring lie'), but he was aware of a strange 'humming'.

All titles must be quoted: that is, they must be either underlined or enclosed by quotation marks.

King Lear is a tragic play.

That is nonsense.

'King Lear' is a tragic play.

So too must all words that you refer to as words.

By and large is a meaningless phrase.

That is nonsense too.

'By and large' is a meaningless phrase.

30 Introducing quotations: doubling the quotation

A student will sometimes introduce a quotation in such a way that he has already quoted it before he has reached it. This practice produces an odd effect – as though the writer were implying: 'There! I've got *that* one in.'

> Chaucer adds the final touch to his description of the Summoner's ugliness by telling us that children were afraid of his face:
> Of his visage children were afeard.

> Chaucer adds the final touch to his description of the Summoner's ugliness by telling us that children were 'afeard' of his 'visage'.

> Brutus tells Cassius that his threats do not frighten him:
> There is no terror, Cassius, in thy threats.

> Brutus replies:
> There is no terror, Cassius, in thy threats.

> Keats longs for a drink of wine –
> O for a draught of vintage!

> Keats longs for a 'draught of vintage'.

> Romeo replies that he has the darkness of the night ('night's cloak') to hide him from Juliet's kinsmen.

> Romeo replies that he has 'night's cloak' to hide him from Juliet's kinsmen.

Lady Macbeth is afraid that her husband's nature is too kind:
  It is too full o' the milk of human kindness.

Lady Macbeth is afraid that her husband's nature is 'too full o' the milk of human kindness'.

The sword flashed in the moonlight –
  Made lightnings in the splendour of the moon.

The sword –
  Made lightnings in the splendour of the moon.

Now rewrite these passages in such a way as to eliminate the 'doubling'. In one of them it may be better to make the quotation flow continuously from the introductory sentence, instead of setting it out on a new line:

Ophelia's clothes (the Queen tells Laertes) spread wide in the water and bore her up, so that she seemed like a mermaid:
  And, mermaid-like, awhile they bore her up.

Caesar declares that he prefers to have fat, contented men about him, and that he distrusts Cassius because he is thin:
  Cassius has a lean and hungry look.

Lawrence describes how the mother kangaroo moves slowly away, almost like a ski-er:
  Goes off in slow sad leaps
  On the long flat skis of her legs.

Roy Campbell relates how he looked round and caught sight of the horses in the distance:
  And, turning, saw afar
  A hundred snowy horses unconfined.

31 Introducing quotations: failing to explain the context

A student will sometimes introduce a quotation too abruptly, without explaining the context:

> Prospero is a deeply imaginative man:
> The cloud-capp'd towers, the gorgeous palaces.

This practice often produces an odd effect too – as though the writer were just casually tossing out the quotation with an air of 'You know – all that jazz.'

> Prospero is a deeply imaginative man. On one occasion, for example, he has a majestic vision of some great civilization – of its 'cloud-capp'd towers' and its 'gorgeous palaces'.

> In the closing scenes of the play Macbeth's nerves and temper become frayed to breaking-point:
> If thou speak'st false
> Upon the next tree shalt thou hang alive.

> In the closing scenes of the play Macbeth's nerves and temper become frayed to breaking-point. For example, when a messenger brings news that Birnam Wood has begun to move, Macbeth turns on him and threatens:
> If thou speak'st false
> Upon the next tree shalt thou hang alive.

> Friar Laurence is a kindly, gentle-mannered man:

What early tongue so sweet saluteth me?

Friar Laurence is a kindly, gentle-mannered man. For example, when Romeo approaches him in the early morning and bids him 'good morrow', the Friar inquires mildly –

What early tongue so sweet saluteth me?

Othello has a majestic dignity:

Keep up your bright swords, for the dew will rust them.

Othello has a majestic dignity. He shows it, for example, in the early part of the play, when with one brief command he silences Brabantio and his followers:

Keep up your bright swords, for the dew will rust them.

32 Introducing quotations: the 'run-through'

When a sentence is continued into a quotation it must be joined to it in such a way that the sense runs through smoothly and logically and grammatically.

> Romeo is filled with wonder when he sees that –
>   . . . here lies Juliet, and her beauty makes
>   This vault a feasting presence full of light.

This is badly arranged: the run-through is neither smooth nor grammatical.

> Romeo is filled with wonder when he looks on Juliet. Her beauty, it seems to him, makes the vault a 'feasting presence full of light'.

> Antony begs Caesar's corpse to forgive him for being –
>
>   . . . meek and gentle with these butchers.
>   Thou art the ruins of the noblest man
>   That ever lived in the tide of times.

The mistake here is not that the quotation has been badly joined to the sentence it completes, but that the second part of it has not been introduced at all.

> Antony begs Caesar's corpse to forgive him for being 'meek and gentle with these butchers'. He goes on to declare:
>   Thou art the ruins of the noblest man
>   That ever lived in the tide of times.

Here are some more examples:

Caliban tells Stephano and Trinculo to –
 Be not afeard; the isle is full of noises,
 Sounds, and sweet airs, that give delight and hurt
 not.

Caliban tells Stephano and Trinculo not to be 'afeard'. The island, he explains, is –
      . . . full of noises,
 Sounds, and sweet airs, that give delight and hurt
 not.

Macbeth announces grimly that 'I have done the deed'.

Macbeth announces grimly that he has 'done the deed'.

Keats pictures autumn sitting by a cyder-press:
 Thou watchest the last oozings hours by hours.

Keats pictures autumn sitting by a cyder-press and watching 'the last oozings hours by hours'.

Ophelia bewails the fact that she –
 Now see that noble and most sovereign reason,
 Like sweet bells jangled, out of tune and harsh.

Ophelia bewails the fact that she now sees –
   . . . that noble and most sovereign reason,
 Like sweet bells jangled, out of tune and harsh.

Wordsworth then asks what song it is that the Highland girl is singing:
 Perhaps the plaintive numbers flow
 For old, unhappy, far-off things. . . .

Wordsworth then asks what song it is that the Highland girl is singing, and he imagines that –

Perhaps the plaintive numbers flow
For old, unhappy, far-off things. . . .

Will you now re-shape these passages, and in each one
make the run-through perfect. In three of them the
quotation is set out on a new line. Possibly, in one or more
of these, it may be better to make it flow continuously from
the introductory sentence:

The King envies all those poor and lowly people who
can sleep peacefully because they are untroubled by
affairs of state, quite different from –
Uneasy lies the head that wears a crown.

Antony, looking on the corpse, can hardly believe
that –
O mighty Caesar! dost thou lie so low?

During a pause in the fighting Macbeth defiantly
shouts out that 'I bear a charmed life'.

Hardy humorously describes Gabriel Oak's smile as
'the corners of his mouth spread till they were within
an unimportant distance of his ears'.

Ted Hughes describes the otter as being –
With webbed feet and long ruddering tail
And a round head like an old tomcat.

33 'Said'

> 'Your best plan', said the old woman, 'is to take the road through the valley.'

Though it is often useful, *said* is lifeless because it is generalized. Sometimes it is better to put a more specific word in place of it. There are plenty available, to suit a wide range of contexts: *declared. . . . insisted. . . . suggested. . . . asserted. . . . hinted. . . . scoffed. . . . protested. . . . grumbled. . . . agreed. . . . persisted. . . . confessed.* Words that describe a sound, especially the less obvious ones, nearly always interpret *said* creatively when they replace it: *mumbled. . . . boomed. . . . brayed. . . . intoned. . . . bleated. . . . whined. . . . laughed. . . . giggled.*

Some words, as well as conveying *said*, also – at one blow, as it were – impart touches of characterisation or description. Words that perform this double task are not easy to come by. Perhaps the speaker had a shiny face, or wore spectacles:

> 'Very well, then,' he gleamed, 'we will do a deal.'

Perhaps someone has had a fit:

> 'Get me the tablets!' he foamed.

Sometimes it is best to cut out all the words that indicate who is speaking and leave it to the quotation marks and the paragraphing to show this. The following extract, for example, which comes from *Right Ho, Jeeves*, by P.G. Wodehouse, would not work at all if 'she said' and 'I replied' were repeated throughout:

> 'You're going to give away the prizes.'
> I goggled. Her words did not appear to make sense.

They seemed the mere aimless vapouring of an aunt who has been sitting out in the sun without a hat.

'Me?'

'You.'

I goggled again.

'You don't mean me?'

'I mean you in person.'

I goggled a third time.

'You're pulling my leg.'

'I am not pulling your leg. Nothing would induce me to touch your beastly leg.'

Now improve the following passage, in two ways. First eliminate all the speaker-indicating words that are superfluous, and secondly, improve on the word *said* each time it appears. There is nothing wrong with *said*, but, as an exercise, rewrite the passage without using a single one. Condense the *said* expressions whenever' possible (for example, 'said in a hesitant tone' could become 'faltered'):

'I must have an answer, son', said the store detective insistently. 'Did you steal it or not?'

'No, I didn't', replied Alan.

'If you didn't', the detective began. . . .

'Don't answer him, Alan', said Jennifer. She faced the detective. 'You've got no right', she told him, 'to question my young brother in that way.'

'If you didn't steal it,' the detective continued, 'what was it doing in your bag?'

'I don't even use that stuff ', said Alan, going red with embarrassment.

'I'll have to ask you both to come with me', said the detective.

'You can ask as much as you like', said Jennifer sharply, 'but we're not prepared to come.'

'In that case', replied the detective, 'I will have to call the police.'

They stood silent. An elderly lady, pushing a trolley, stared briefly as she passed.

'Well?' inquired the detective.

'It rather looks, doesn't it,' said Jennifer in a sulky manner, 'as though we haven't got much choice.'

34 Sentences that end strongly

When we write a sentence the natural thing to do is to put the main point first because it is uppermost in our mind, and then we add whatever else we want to say:

> The little village of Bream lay half a mile further on, just out of sight behind a screen of hazel and ash.

We do not have to follow this natural arrangement. We can keep the main point till the end:

> Half a mile further on, just out of sight behind a screen of hazel and ash, lay the little village of Bream.

A writer's purpose, when he shapes a sentence in that way, is to build up a sense of expectation, so that when he finally does come out with his main point it has an added force. This is a useful technical device to keep in mind if you want to sharpen the emphasis of a statement:

> Lies of this sort poison the mind, from whatever quarter they come, and however plausibly they may be presented.

> Lies of this sort, from whatever quarter they come, and however plausibly they may be presented, poison the mind.

It is useful, too, if you want to heighten the drama of some event you are describing:

> Suddenly he stood still and listened. A child was calling

from far away, with a cry so faint that he could only just catch the sound of it.

Suddenly he stood still and listened. From far away, with a cry so faint that he could only just catch the sound of it, a child was calling.

Here are some pieces of writing by various authors. In each passage I have altered one of the sentences by rearranging the order of the words. The authors ended these sentences strongly, with the main point in each case being kept back till the end. I have put the main point at the beginning or near the beginning. Will you look through each passage, decide which sentence has been altered, and then rewrite that sentence as the author wrote it. Change only the word order, not the words themselves. A few minor adjustments to the punctuation may be needed.

There was a silence on the river as the *Swallow* drifted on. 'I see it! I see it!' cried Roger. On the front of the boathouse was a huge skull-and-cross bones, high up over the entrance, cut out of wood and painted staring white. (Arthur Ransome, *Swallows and Amazons*)

One afternoon the Rector appeared in the doorway when a pitched battle was raging among the big boys in the class, and the mistress was calling imploringly for order. 'Silence!' he roared. The silence was immediate and profound, for they knew he was not to be trifled with. (Flora Thompson, *Lark Rise to Candleford*)

The pack hunted the otter, between boulders and rocks crusted with shellfish and shaggy with seaweed, and past worm-channered posts that marked the fairway for fishing boats at high water. Off each post a gull launched itself, cackling angrily as it looked down at the animals. (Henry Williamson *Tarka the Otter*)

He had promised me a silver fourpenny on the first of every month if I would keep my eye open for a seafaring man with one leg, and let him know the moment he appeared. But often enough he would only blow through his nose at me and stare me down, when the first of the month came round and I applied to him for my wage. (R.L. Stevenson, *Treasure Island*)

Many people regarded the Chancellor as a mouse when he took office last January. But already he has become a major political figure, just six months later, to the astonishment of everyone. (From a newspaper article)

The correct versions of these passages are given on page 125.

35 Parentheses which improve sentences

A parenthesis is a word, or a group of words, that has been set aside from the main flow of a sentence by being enclosed between a pair of punctuation marks. The marks may be a pair of commas, a pair of dashes, or a pair of brackets. We use commas for this purpose very often. They set the words aside in the lightest possible way:

A stranger, perhaps, would not have noticed it.

Her mother, she knew, would be beginning to worry.

These two sentences, with their simple, natural-sounding parentheses, flow pleasingly.

The secret, often, of giving a sentence a shape or a rhythm is to have a parenthesis in it.

The following sentence reads like a continuous jet. To put it another way: the reader, although he is being made to do quite a long journey, is not given a single breather:

Every scholar who has studied Marlowe's life has had to resign himself to the fact that the answer to this question and probably to many others too lies sealed up forever in Shakespeare's tomb at Stratford.

Every scholar who has studied Marlowe's life has had to resign himself to the fact that the answer to this question, and probably to many others too, lies sealed up forever in Shakespeare's tomb at Stratford.

A parenthesis will help.

It seems that the letter which has recently been found proves him to be completely innocent of some of the more serious charges that were laid against him when he occupied the post of Vice-President.

This sentence, unlike the previous one, has no hidden parenthesis around which commas could be put. So we will rearrange the order of the words in such a way as to give it one:

The letter which has recently been found proves him to be completely innocent, it seems, of some of the more serious charges that were laid against him when he occupied the post of Vice-President.

In each of the following sentences two of the commas which the author put in, to form a parenthesis, could have been left out, and in the version given here they have been. Will you write out the sentences, putting back into each one the two missing commas. Notice, in each case, the improvement that is brought about in the shape of the sentence. They all come from *Treasure Island*:

He was hunched as if with age or weakness and he wore a huge old tattered sea-cloak with a hood.

It was a bitter cold winter with hard frosts and heavy gales and it was plain from the first that my poor father was unlikely to see the spring.

Right in front of me not half a mile away I beheld the Hispaniola under sail.

I had quite made up my mind that the mutineers after their repulse that morning had nothing nearer their hearts than to up anchor and away to sea.

The sentences in the next group have been altered in a different way. The words that Stevenson had originally put in parenthesis – enclosed between commas during the course of the sentences – have been moved to the beginning. Here is an example:

> Therefore it was plain that the attack would be developed from the north.

Stevenson wrote:

> It was plain, therefore, that the attack would be developed from the north.

Will you now rewrite each of the following sentences as Stevenson wrote them.

> As you may fancy, I was very uneasy and alarmed and it rather added to my fears to observe that the stranger was certainly frightened himself.

> For his part the captain stood staring at the signboard like a bewildered man.

> I think it went sorely with all of us to leave those men there in that wretched state.

> By this time I had taken such a horror of his cruelty that I could scarce conceal a shudder when he laid his hand upon my arm.

The original versions of these four sentences are quoted on page 126.

36 Parentheses which spoil sentences

> These minor characters add a touch of humour to, and relieve the sadness of, the play.

The parenthesis wrenches this sentence into an unnatural shape. It is quite unnecessary:

> These minor characters add a touch of humour to the play and relieve the sadness of it.

> These ancient tombs have never been, and it is probable that they never will be, found.

'Found', here, falls on the ear like a dud note.

> These ancient tombs have never been found and probably never will be.

Careless writers who wedge a parenthesis in the middle of a verb often stumble into a grammatical error:

> These ancient tombs have never, and probably never will be, found.

A jolt will always be liable to occur if a parenthesis is inserted immediately after a word that has a strong tendency to lead straight on:

> This producer, who, as *The Times* critic noted, already has a distinguished career behind him, shows a strong respect for, and never tries to modernise, Shakespeare's work.

This is a bleakly pedantic way of writing.

No doubt there are times when for some reason or other it may be necessary to write a sentence which has a jolt in it. But some writers do it when there is no need to. They seem to enjoy it.

Will you now rearrange these sentences in such a way that they flow smoothly:

> This way of tackling the job introduces more pleasure into, and relieves the monotony of, the work.

> He should have, and on one occasion nearly did, become Prime Minister.

> He is a man who, if he is left alone, will be likely, in my opinion, to work wonders for the firm.

Now rewrite the following sentence twice: first, as it stands but with the grammatical mistake in it eliminated; then in such a way as to make it flow more smoothly:

> Although this story could, and often has been, told at length, we can only summarise it here.

37 Misleading sentences

A writer, guiding his readers along the path of a sentence, should never lead them down a false trail. On the contrary, he should make sure that every step is clear.

> While he waited and watched the window on the opposite side of the street, which was black with grime, kept banging and swinging.

The reader is tripped up. He has to withdraw his attention, momentarily, from what the writer is saying, in order to sort out the muddle.

> As soon as they came out into the open smoke, mixed with gas and other fumes, began to pour out of the building.

The above examples are made up. The following are not:

> All round him the long scar smashed into the jungle was a bath of heat. (William Golding, *Lord of the Flies*)

> Then she bent down and washed her hands and her wedding-ring – which was loose anyhow – began to slip off. (Edna O'Brien *August is a Wicked Month*)

It might be thought that hitches like these are too trifling to be worth mentioning. But they are irritating. And anyway, what is wrong with aiming at perfection? 'Perfection', wrote Michelangelo, 'is achieved by attending to innumerable trifles; but perfection itself is no trifle.'

Now improve the following sentences, either by changing the order of the words in such a way as to form parentheses, or else by altering the punctuation. Do not change any of the words:

As the fog thickened the air in the valley took on a trance-like stillness.

As soon as the curtain had been drawn across the Mayor, who was in the front row, rose to speak.

He felt a longing for a moment, as he walked away, to turn back.

He has suffered from what I can gather, since early childhood, from a form of mental instability.

These passages read beautifully by John Betjeman had a strange appeal.

It happened that on this occasion he was accompanied by a stroke of good fortune by the very person I had been wanting to meet.

38 *Adjectives that contribute nothing*

'Be a miser with adjectives', wrote Eden Phillpots. It is good advice, for they are words which can very easily slip into a person's writing when they are not needed and weaken it.

> I admired his tremendous courage.... We were entranced by the wonderful beauty of the scene.... I still remember the excitement I felt when I first read this interesting story.

All the adjectives do, in these sentences, is add superfluous comments. If you read the sentences again and leave them out, you will see the improvement.

There is a simple stratagem you could try out (which nearly always works) if you are looking for a way to improve something you have written. Go through it and cross out all the adjectives which you have used merely in order to enrich what you are saying, and which are not essential to the meaning.

> One of the most difficult and dangerous climbs in the whole world is the ascent of the forbidding south-west face of Everest. A treacherous surface, continual blizzards, a thin atmosphere – these are some of the terrible hazards which a climber of these bleak slopes has to face.

> One of the most difficult climbs in the world is the ascent of the south-west face of Everest. A treacherous surface, continual blizzards, a thin atmosphere – these

are some of the hazards which a climber of these slopes has to face.

It is not being suggested – it would be absurd to – that all enriching adjectives should be banned from writing, merely that since weak ones can so easily be slipped in, they should be rigorously screened. Here is a paragraph from *The Slave*, by Isaac Bashevis Singer. The adjectives are printed in italics:

The sun had moved westward; the day was nearing its end. The sky was still *clear*, but a *milk-white* fog was forming in the woods. Jacob could see for miles around. The mountains remained as *deserted* as in the days of the Creation. One above the other, the forests rose, first the *leaf-bearing* trees, and then the pines and the firs.

All those adjectives except one were introduced by the author not to enrich his description, but because he needed them in order to be able to say what he wanted to say. Which one did he introduce to enrich the picture?

In this next extract from *The Slave*, the author used two adjectives. I have spoilt it by adding five more – all of them superfluous. Will you rewrite it as he wrote it, without my adjectives. Then read through what you have written and see how much better it is without them:

It stormed in the middle of the night. A sudden flash of lightning lit up the interior of the barn, and the cows, dung heaps, and earthen pots became visible for a brief instant. Thunder rumbled, and a strong gust of wind blew open the barn door. The heavy downpour beat on the roof like hail. The driving rain lashed Jacob as he closed and latched the door. He built a small fire, and sat by it, praying.

This extract and the two that follow are quoted correctly on page 126.

In the next passage three superfluous adjectives have been added to what Isaac Bashevis Singer originally wrote. Which three?

> After a while the wagon entered a beautiful pine-wood, which seemed less a forest than some heavenly mansion. The trees were as tall and straight as pillars, and the sky leaned on their green tops. The light which filtered through shone with all the various colours of the rainbow. Jacob closed his eyes as though begrudging himself the sight of such great splendour.

Which are the two that have been added to the following passage?

> Wandering through the narrow street, Jacob saw how great the poverty was. Many lived in what were only dark burrows; tradesmen worked in shops that looked like wretched kennels. A horrible stench rose from the gutters.

39 Padding

There could be no doubt that Walter was a terribly self-conscious type of person. When there was a party going on and everyone in the room started singing songs or something like that, he never really joined in with the fun because he couldn't ever bring himself to join in. It was just not in his nature. He sat there smiling round at everyone all the time to show he was pleased, but it was perfectly obvious to all those present that his smile was only put on because you could see it was forced.

The passage above is a spoilt version of something that was written by Somerset Maugham. This is what he wrote:

Walter was self-conscious. When there was a party going on and everyone started singing, he could never bring himself to join in. He sat there smiling to show he was pleased, but his smile was forced.

If you use more words than are needed to say something, you weaken the force of your writing. You also try the patience of your reader. A good writer weighs up what he writes, and he takes care not to include in it anything that is empty or trivial or repetitious. That is not to say that he never allows himself a lightweight sentence here and there, or a little word like *very* or *rather*. These are relaxations, and he allows them in if they help his writing to flow. But he eliminates any wordiness that spoils it.

People can never write too sparely. It is not possible to, because economy of style is not a fault. Here is a piece of advice. If you are ever in any doubt as to whether something is worth including or not, do not include it.

The following passages are padded out versions of pieces of writing by well-known authors. Will you rewrite them, leaving out any words that you think are superfluous. Do not make any other changes (except adjustments to the punctuation). The number of words that have been added is given in brackets at the end of each passage. You will find the authors' original versions on page 127.

> Macalister's boy took one of the fish and cut a whole square piece out of its side to bait the hook with. The poor creature's mutilated body (it was alive still, even after having had that done to it) was thrown back into the sea to die a lingering death. (Virginia Woolf, *To the Lighthouse* – 17 words added)

> In the morning they buried Mrs Collard. The serjeant got a coolie, and he dug a shallow grave to lay her in. When it was ready they lowered her into it covered with a blanket, and Mrs Horsefall read a little out of the Prayer Book. Then, when she had finished, they took away the blanket so that it should not get buried, because they could not spare that, and the earth was filled in over Mrs Collard's body. (Nevil Shute, *A Town Like Alice* – 23 words added)

Now here is a passage which has not been changed. It appears as Barbara Cartland wrote it in *The Dream and the Glory*:

> Then, as if he could not help himself or resist the invitation of Cordelia's arms, his mouth came down on hers. He was trying to be gentle; he was trying, she knew, to keep control of himself. But a flame within her seemed to leap higher and as it rose it ignited a fire in him, so that his kisses became fierce, demanding, masterful, and wildly passionate.

40 Jargon

Jargon is the pretentious language of a person who likes to be regarded as an expert. There is no kind of language that spreads faster. Some impressive-sounding word or phrase is put forward by someone and soon it gets taken up and parroted by others, who welcome it as a short cut to expertise. It then becomes fixed as the phrase that is always used, without thought, to make some particular point:

> This approach is counter-productive.

Counter-productive is a clumsy word; it is not specific; and it is self-contradicting. (How can anything *counter-produce* anything?) However, it is the stock adjective.

Jargon, by its nature, since its aim is to impress, is full of muddled thinking:

> This course provides the parameters within which the changing facets of the work can be accommodated.

Does it mean, 'This is a varied course'?

A careful writer, who is trying to say something which is not easy to express, will search and search until he finds the simplest possible way of putting it. The very search, as he well knows, will often shape and clarify his thinking. The purveyor of jargon is not concerned with any of that; for what he is really doing is using the language as a means of promoting his career.

41 Step by step, sentence by sentence

It is nearly always best, if you have a passage of reasoning to unfold, to divide it into stages and have a separate sentence for each stage. People sometimes pour out, in one go, quite long stretches of argument – probably because the points all come into their minds at once and they feel they have to get them down quickly, before they slip away:

> In my opinion those people who blame the violence of modern society on the bad influence of television and say that the violent scenes in television films encourage violence in real life are wrong, because art is a reflection of life and those films only reflect an attitude that already exists and are not the cause of it.

It may be a good idea to write the argument down like that, but it will only be a rough draft. The writer should look at it again and try to improve it by dividing it up, so that the argument will be unfolded step by step, in separate sentences.

> Some people blame the violence of modern society on the bad influence of television. The violent scenes in television films, they say, encourage violence in real life. In my opinion they are wrong. For art is a reflection of life, and those films only reflect an attitude that already exists: they are not the cause of it.

Will you now improve the following passage, in the same way as we improved the previous one, by dividing it into either three, four, or five sentences:

Although a group of people, who are undoubtedly sincere, have recently mounted a campaign to get film censorship abolished, since they regard it as an interference with the liberty of the individual, it would, in my opinion, be a serious mistake to abolish it, because other values need protection as well as liberty, such as children, who need to be protected from the horrifying scenes that occur in some films.

Notice and eliminate the flaw that comes near the end: *children* are not *values*.

Now improve the following passage by dividing it into six sentences. If you make the second and third ones very short, and the fourth, by contrast, long, you will end up with a well-shaped paragraph:

Gliding will never become a popular sport, for two reasons, first because it is expensive, a modern glider being a complicated machine, with a full panel of instruments, a radio link, airbrakes, an oxygen supply, and several other devices, which means that only a rich person can afford to possess one, and secondly because it is a sport with a strong element of loneliness and danger in it.

42 For and against

When you are putting forward an argument in favour of some point of view, you may want to mention the objections that can be raised against it, so that you can dismiss them. It is usually best to mention these first; then you can end by affirming the rightness of the point of view you favour. It is not good to dodge about from one side of the argument to the other:

> The television film of *David Copperfield* was a fine production, but the fact remains that seeing the film of a classic is no substitute for reading the book, but the film must have given many people who would never read Dickens some idea of what his writing is like.

In the passage above, the first *but* turns the reader's thoughts away from the opening line of argument, and a moment later the second *but* turns them back to it. This switching about will be avoided if we arrange the ideas more logically and first deal with the two points that stand against the opinion we are putting forward:

> The television film of *David Copperfield* was a fine production and it must have given many people who would never read Dickens some idea of what his writing is like. But the fact remains that seeing the film of a classic is no substitute for reading the book.

Now improve these passages. Each one has the same kind of fault – a double switch:

> I prefer to do my shopping in small shops, although in a big store it is possible to buy everything under one

roof, because in small shops they give you a personal service. (One sentence)

I believe that a God of some kind must exist, but I do not believe in the conventional God-in-the-sky figure, because it seems to me that there is no other way of explaining life. (One sentence)

Lord of the Flies is a study of human nature, but on the surface it might seem to be nothing more than a book about violence and cruelty, but at a deeper level it is a study of the different ways in which people might behave if they were freed from social restrictions. (Two sentences – the second one short)

I disagree with the view of some people who want to put a stop to the exploration of space and consider that it is too costly and maintain that the money would be better spent on such undertakings as medical research or the relief of poverty, because the exploration of space is an outlet for man's spirit of adventure, and life would not be worth living if this spirit were stifled. (Four sentences – the third one consisting of two words)

43 Imagery: similes

We introduce imagery into our writing whenever we compare one thing to another in an imaginative way.

The moon looked like a silver coin.

Imagery is created by means of similes or metaphors. If a writer makes a comparison in a straightforward manner, and just says quite openly that one thing looks like another one, he is using a simile. 'Like a silver coin' is a simile.

The moon was sailing through the clouds as swiftly and smoothly as a ship.

This, too, is a simile, because it is a straightforward comparison.

Similes nearly always include the words *like* or *as*. Metaphors never do. The difference, as we shall see when we come to metaphors, goes deeper than that.

When a writer uses a simile his imagination never overwhelms the reality. 'The moon looked like a silver coin.' The person who wrote that did not suppose, even for a moment, that the moon *was* a silver coin. A simile rules out an imaginative leap of that kind. If you think the moon is *like* a silver coin you cannot think it *is* one.

Do you think that any of the similes in the following pieces of writing are poor in any way? (Are they sentimental, perhaps, or ridiculous, or too obvious, or inappropriate?) It might be thought that two or three are, possibly four. If you think any are, indicate which by writing down the first two or three words of the extract and then explain why you think so. You can find out the names of the authors, if you wish to, by turning to page 127. (Do not look until you have expressed your opinion.)

The drive twisted and turned like an enchanted ribbon through the dark and silent woods.

She primmed her mouth tighter and tighter, puckering it as if it were sewed.

The timbered cottage, with its sloping, cloak-like roof, was old and forgotten.

He pulled her close against him and his lips came down on hers. It was a feeling so perfect that it was as if she had kissed the sunlight.

The keyboard of the piano looked like a mouthful of bad teeth, chipped, yellow, and some missing altogether.

He looked at the sky and saw the white cumulus built like friendly piles of ice cream.

Before them, but some distance off, there stood a green hill-top, treeless, rising like a bald head out of the encircling wood.

In the following passages (from *I Can't Stay Long*, by Laurie Lee), blank spaces have been left where the author had used similes. Suggest a simile (of one word or more) to fill each space, then turn to page 127 and compare yours with his:

In Florence the spring was over and the heat had come. The carved palaces quivered like —— in the sun.

The road was white and deep with dust. The dust lifted like —— on the evening wind and coated my hair and hands with tiny fragments of marble – marble of the Tuscan cities and their white cathedrals.

I found a wood at last and unpacked. I rolled myself up in my bag and tried to sleep. The moon came up over the trees and shone into my face like a ——.

I took the road once more. The sun was inexorable, the landscape already quivering like —— in the heat.

That night I camped on a high plain, on a platform of ground commanding great views. When the blue night came, the distances below me, with their many villages, sprang into clusters of light, like ——.

Siena stood far off, but clear, a proper city, rose-red and ringed by a great wall. And behind it hung a folded mountain, blue, like ——.

44 Metaphors

The moon was a ghostly galleon, tossed upon cloudy
seas.

This is not a simile. The writer does not say that the moon
was *like* a ghostly galleon: he has allowed his imagination to
carry him further than that. To him, when he wrote that
sentence – for we must take him at his word – the moon *was* a
ghostly galleon. When a writer declares, in that way, that two
different things are one and the same, he is using a
metaphor.

In the metaphor the writer mentions the moon. So the
idea of it, as a reality, was present at the back of his mind
when he wrote the sentence. It is possible to go further, and
not mention it at all:

I looked up and saw that the silver ship of the night was
already sailing the sky.

Here, the writer's imagination has taken him still further
away from reality. For a moment, while the spell lasted, the
moon ceased to exist, and he saw only a silver ship. His vision,
as he wrote those words, was so completely dominated by his
imagination that the image overwhelmed the reality and put
it out of his mind, so that he did not even mention it. A
metaphor like this one is the very opposite of a simile. In a
simile it is the reality that predominates.

So we could say that there are two kinds of metaphor. One
includes a reference to the reality it pictures and therefore it
only partially eclipses it:

The moon rose – a gaunt skull.

105

The other, more deeply imaginative, blots the reality out, not mentioning it all, so that for a moment the image, or picture, becomes the reality:

A gaunt skull began to show through the clouds.

Now turn the following metaphors into similes. Here is an example:

The lanterns had thrown a bright necklace round the lake.

The lanterns encircled the lake like a bright necklace.

Change the next two in a similar way.

The burnt oil had laid a black cloak over the sand.

Out to sea, beyond the headland, a rock raised a giant fist above the water.

Now turn the following simile into a metaphor. All you need do is leave out five consecutive words.

Towards the west, on the horizon, dark clouds were beginning to fill the sky with their shapes, which were like towers and battlements.

Change the next one into a metaphor by leaving out four consecutive words.

The vine had thrust its tendrils, which were like tiny claws, through the cracks in the window-frame.

Here are some more similes for you to turn into metaphors. The numbers in brackets indicate the number of words needed in the metaphors.

The sun was hurling down dazzling rays of light, like spears. (7)

The process of urbanisation has almost engulfed this stretch of old common-land, like a tide. (12)

We pushed forward into the thorn-covered bushes, hacking our way through tangles that pressed round us like barbed-wire. (13)

The lightning flashed across the sky as though tearing a crevice in it. (8)

45 'Of' metaphors

A sea of corn. . . . A pillar of smoke. . . . A yellow kite of a moon. . . . The rocket exploded into a tree of sparks. . . . The lantern laid a ladder of rosy light across the water. . . .

'I stared at the pillar of smoke.' What was I looking at – a pillar or smoke? A pillar; but it was made of smoke. The image dominates the reality.

'I stared at the smoke, which rose up like a pillar.' What was I looking at? The smoke; but it reminded me of a pillar. The reality dominates the image.

There lies the difference between a metaphor and a simile. In the one the image is dominant; in the other, the reality.

Here are four descriptions of the earth, seen from the air. In the first two it is seen during the daytime, in the last two at night:

He was about a thousand feet up, and he looked down and saw flat green country with fields and hedges and no trees. He could see some cows in the field below him. (Roald Dahl, *Over to you*)

Bond had a moment of exhilaration as the sun came up. Twenty thousand feet below, the houses began to show like grains of sugar spilt across a brown carpet. Nothing moved on the earth's surface except a thin worm of smoke from a train, the straight white feather of a fishing boat's wake across an inlet, and the glint of chromium from a toy motor car caught in the sun. (Ian Fleming, *Diamonds are Forever*)

A moment later they were flying only fifty feet above

the roof-tops of the town. They could spot scattered lights below them, as the black-out was anything but perfect. The glow from the snow, which was broken by black patches, enabled them to pick out the principal buildings. (Dennis Wheatley, *Faked Passports*)

The first lights showed below us – long ribbons of amber, orange, white and blue. And then the great sprawling mass of the city seen only as slashes of arterial brilliance, the blank spaces in between dotted with the pinpoints of individual street lights like thousands upon thousands of tiny perforations in a black sheet of paper. (Hammond Innes, *The Strode Venturer*)

A skilful use of imagery forms the very essence of good descriptive writing. Two of these four passages are enriched by it and two are not. As an experiment will you rewrite the two that are merely factual in such a way as to introduce some imagery into them. Do not add very much: just a few touches will make all the difference.

46 Metaphors that reside in the verb

Another way of forming a metaphor is to convey the image in the verb. It is a very neat and economical way. 'Rain pimpled the pavement', wrote a poet, taking four words to say something for which a lesser writer would have needed ten or twenty.

> Spray rose from the tops of the waves. . . . steamed from the tops of the waves. A clump of reeds grew in a corner of the pond. . . . spiked a corner of the pond. Hundreds of parachutes dotted the sky. . . . tattooed the sky. Snow covered the fields. . . . sheeted the fields. At the back of the grate a yellow flame appeared. . . . flowered.

Here are four similes. Turn each one into a metaphor, in such a way that the imagery is confined to a single word – the verb. The number of words needed for each sentence is given in brackets. For example:

> The church spire thrust itself into the sky like a spear. (6)

> The church spire speared the sky.

> The wounded snake twitched like a whip into the undergrowth. (7)

> Sweat appeared on his face like beads. (4)

> Frost lay on the grass like fur. (4)

The tower was surmounted by a green dome, which looked like a cap on it. (8)

Now make each of the following sentences metaphorical by changing the verb (and also, if you want to, the preposition that goes with it):

His cheeks were covered with hair.

The hull of the wreck was covered with barnacles.

He lay back; the little mound of grass supported his head.

One of the distant summits was topped by an ancient fort.

A dense fog lay over the city.

47 Personification

A writer personifies inanimate objects – that is, he suggests that they are living beings.

Personification is imagery. It must therefore take the form of either a simile or a metaphor, for only they can bring an image into being.

We will first personify the moon by means of a simile:

A silent moon was gazing down at us, like a pale-faced nun.

Now, by means of a metaphor:

> A sickly leper of a moon had climbed above the roof-tops.

And finally by means of that deeper kind of metaphor in which the reality is blotted out and not mentioned:

> A radiant queen was walking the night.

Similes show up, but metaphors often slip by unnoticed. All these sentences contain personifications, some conspicuous, some scarcely noticeable:

> The sun shone unmercifully. . . . A cruel sea pounded the wreck. . . . The floorboards groaned under the weight. . . . The wind had herded the leaves into a corner of the yard. . . . A solitary tower-block, silhouetted against the clouds, braved the storm. . . . Along the edge of the forest the leaves whispered. . . . The machine grunted and mumbled before finally coughing out the printed copy. . . . The wind moaned in the chimney. . . .

Now look at the following passages, which come from

Rebecca, by Daphne du Maurier, and write down all the words that contribute to the personifications:

> A lilac had mated with a copper beech, and to bind them yet more closely to one another the malevolent ivy, always an enemy to grace, had thrown her tendrils about the pair and made them prisoners.

> I looked out, and I saw below me the smooth grass lawns stretching to the sea, and the sea itself, bright green with white-tipped crests, whipped by a westerly wind. A hurrying cloud hid the sun for a moment as I watched, and the sea changed colour instantly, becoming black, and the white crests very pitiless suddenly, and cruel.

> The room would bear witness to our presence. The little heap of library books marked ready to return, and the discarded copy of *The Times*; ashtrays, with the stub of a cigarette; cushions, with the imprint of our heads upon them, lolling in the chairs; the charred embers of our log fire still smouldering.

Now introduce a personification into each of the following sentences by changing the verb (and also, if you want to, the preposition that goes with it):

> The kite, as it rose, began to flap in the wind.

> The pneumatic drill bored through the concrete.

> A violent gust blew through the empty barn.

> He put a log on the fire and watched as a thin blue flame began to draw round it.

> The exhaust emitted black smoke.

> The harbour lights shone in the water.

113

The burning plane had left a line of black smoke across the sky.

The sun moved slowly through the clouds.

Though she tried to dismiss her suspicions a thought remained at the back of her mind.

He pressed the lever, and the pump began to pour the oil into the can.

48 Sustained metaphors

Sometimes, in a descriptive passage, a writer will sustain just one image through several sentences. He will explore it and elaborate on it, trying to find within it more and more resemblances to what he is describing – almost (one feels sometimes) as though he has challenged himself to find as many as possible.

In *Lord of the Flies* William Golding explores the similarities between a fire on a mountainside and a devouring animal:

> Small flames stirred at the bole of the tree and crawled away through leaves and brushwood, dividing and increasing. One patch touched a tree trunk and scrambled up like a bright squirrel. The smoke increased, sifted, rolled outwards. The squirrel leapt on the wings of the wind and clung to another standing tree, eating downwards. Beneath the dark canopy of leaves and smoke the fire laid hold on the forest and began to gnaw. Acres of black and yellow smoke rolled steadily towards the sea. At the sight of the flames the boys broke into shrill, excited cheering. The flames crept as a jaguar creeps on its belly towards a line of birch-like saplings.

A sustained metaphor nearly always includes similes. The term really denotes sustained imagery.

If a metaphor is extended even slightly, it begins to take on the character of a sustained one. In *Tarka the Otter* Henry Williamson wrote:

> At the tail of the pool the river quickened smoothly into paws of water. . . .

Having given the water paws, he gave the paws claws:

> . . . . quickened smoothly into paws of water, with star-streaming claws.

Will you now alter the second part of these sentences in such a way that it extends the image that has been created in the first part. The words to be replaced are in italics. What you will create, in each case, is a sustained metaphor in embryo. Here is an example:

> A single cloud was sailing like some great ship across an *area* of blue sky.

> A single cloud was sailing like some great ship across an *ocean* of blue sky.

> Like an actress leaving the stage the moon drew back behind the *bank* of clouds.

> The plane looked like a giant fish, stranded on a wide *expanse* of tarmac.

> From the top of the palace walls, which rose sheer, like white cliffs, one could look out across the vast *stretch* of the western desert.

> Thousands of feet below he saw the glowing brooch that was the city centre; and to the south of it, stretching away into the night, the *line* of lights that marked the course of the motorway.

Now write a descriptive passage, of about the same length as the extract from *Lord of the Flies*, based on a single sustained metaphor. Choose whatever subject-matter and whatever image you like; but if you want some suggestions here are three:

116

Describe the view from a boat in a rough sea, and let your description be dominated by an image of mountains. In other words, interpret the sea as a mountainous place, with lofty peaks, precipitous slopes, snow-caps, avalanches, and so on.

Describe a wood in terms of a cathedral – from the point of view, perhaps, of someone walking through it.

Describe a foggy street as though it were an underwater scene – again, perhaps, from the point of view of someone walking along it or driving along it.

Do not try to include metaphors or similes in every sentence of your description. That would overload it. Let some of them be factual, as a contrast.

49 Simile, metaphor, and personification

Here is a description of a sunrise, from *Death in Venice*, by Thomas Mann:

> At the world's edge began a strewing of roses, a shining and a blooming ineffably pure. Baby cloudlets hung illuminated, like attendant cupids, in the blue and blushful haze. Purple effulgence fell upon the sea, that seemed to heave it forward on its welling waves. From horizon to zenith went quivering thrusts, like golden lances. The gleam became a glare. Without a sound, with god-like violence, glow and glare and rolling flames streamed upwards, and with flying hoof-beats the steeds of the sun-god mounted the sky.

As would be expected in a deeply imaginative passage, it is on metaphor that the writer chiefly relies. For, as we have seen, metaphors, unlike similes, overwhelm the reality from which they are derived, and replace it with their own imaginary reality.

At the world's edge began a strewing of roses. This metaphor can be read as a factual statement, and it is meant to be. The reason it can be is that the reality lying behind it (the brightening pink colours in the dawn sky) is not mentioned, and therefore the fact that it is an image is not revealed.

With flying hoof-beats the steeds of the sun-god mounted the sky. This sentence suggests one way of defining the word metaphor: pictorial fantasy presented as fact.

50 Mixed Metaphors

> I had sunk into a deep morass of despair, and although my friends tried to comfort me I could see no light at the end of it.

Mixed metaphors can be funny. The humour does not just lie in their absurdity, but also in the fact that the writer or speaker remains comically unaware that he has said anything funny at all:

> That argument was a complete red herring, and yet you swallowed it whole. I was surprised.

> These scandals had about them the stench of corruption, and rumours were beginning to spread. But the new Secretary-General managed to bottle it up.

Many of the mixed metaphors that one comes across in writing are not likely to be as blundering as these. Most writers are not so careless as to bundle together, in a ridiculous way, two incompatible images. But there is another trap, which is much easier to fall into – the mistake of setting up an image and then making it do something it cannot do:

> Suddenly, with a loud huzza, a little cloud of pirates leapt from the woods on the north side, and ran straight for the stockade. (From *Treasure Island*)

Stevenson's little cloud has not only to jump and run, but also to give out a cheer.

> Barbara Cartland also fell into the trap:

> It was a room, she thought, that might have stepped straight out of a fairy-story.

A room with legs?

Rewrite the following sentences in such a way as to 'unmix' the metaphors. In each sentence there are two metaphors that do not go together. Either change one so that it conforms with the other, or else replace one of them with a literal statement.

As an example, consider the sentence that is quoted at the beginning of page 119. We could write 'I had entered a dark tunnel of despair, and although my friends tried to comfort me I could see no light at the end of it'; or 'I had sunk into a deep morass of despair, and although my friends tried to comfort me I felt that I would never cease to be miserable'.

The shadow of a smile lit up his face.

In those days many people felt that they were standing on the threshold of a new chapter in human history.

There was a searchlight battery on the headland, and long pencils of light towered up through the darkness.

It was his aim to keep this skeleton-in-the-cupboard concealed from everyone, but before long his neighbours began to get wind of it.

Heavy clouds began to blow across our path, and soon we were bathed in a wall of mist.

He extended the hand of friendship to these people, but all they did was throw it back in his face.

A gulf divided the two factions, and there seemed to be no way of overcoming it.

This poisonous remark wounded her deeply.

Now make up three sentences that show examples of mixed

metaphors. Make the blunders believable, as if someone really might have made them.

Finally, make up three mixed metaphors which contain unintended humour.

51 Dead metaphors

A dead metaphor is one that has been used so often that the picture it once conjured up has been worn away:

> He barged into the room. . . . A ray of hope. . . . She saw it in a new light. . . . He was dogged by bad luck. . . . The crux of the matter. . . . To undermine a person's confidence. . . . To ride roughshod over other people's feelings. . . . On the brink of war. . . . He avoided the usual pitfalls. . . . To spin a yarn. . . .

In just these few expressions there is a wealth of pictorial imagery, but constant use has obliterated it all.

The language is full of dead metaphors. There is nothing wrong with them. Many of them have become the accepted way of saying something. But now, because their pictures have faded, it seems that all they are doing is making a literal statement.

Make up four sentences and include in each one a dead metaphor connected with either an animal or a bird. There is one example amongst those we have just looked at. Here is one more: 'He craned his neck out of the window'.

Now make up three more sentences, and include in each one a dead metaphor in which a feature of the landscape is associated with a part of the human body. For example: 'the mouth of the river'.

52 Forced imagery

Metaphors and similes offer such an obvious way of improving one's writing that people are sometimes tempted to introduce one or other of them, not because they need it to enrich or clarify their meaning, but because they think it sounds impressive.

> Orwell brings the sharp razor-edge of his wit to bear on this pretentious nonsense.

> It is through this weak link in Othello's steel personality that Iago stabs.

> The powerful strokes with which he paints his word-pictures.

> This story of violence and passion ends on a peaceful note, like the quiet harmonies that die away as they bring some turbulent symphony to a close.

These images, one feels, were conceived and elaborated as examples of 'good writing'. For this reason they sound amateurish and insincere.

> Agatha Christie's characters spring up from the page like the cardboard cut-outs in a child's story-book.

The simile is not needed. The writer simply meant:

> Agatha Christie's characters are cardboard figures.

Always use imagery sincerely – that is to say, introduce a metaphor or a simile only if you think it will enhance or clarify what you are trying to convey, and never because you think it will sound impressive as a piece of writing.

Epilogue

Students whose standard of written English is poor will not be able to set out an intelligent argument, no matter what subject they are writing about; for they will not be able to think clearly. A thought only becomes clear when it is expressed in clear language. The very process of searching for the most accurate way of expressing it shapes it and modifies it.

What about students who, though the general standard of their writing may be poor, are yet gifted imaginatively? If they are writing an imaginative passage, will not that gift overcome their technical shortcomings? They will not be able to do it justice. For an imaginative idea, though it may have been conceived in a flash of insight, only takes shape as the writer struggles to find the best way of putting it down on paper; and the more assured his mastery of the technical means available, the more vivid he will be able to make it.

It is important, therefore, that students should learn to improve the technique of their writing, for that is one of the surest ways of improving its content.

Correct versions of extracts

Page 82

On the front of the boathouse, high up over the entrance, cut out of wood and painted staring white, was a huge skull-and-cross-bones. (Arthur Ransome)

Page 82

One afternoon, when a pitched battle was raging among the big boys in the class and the mistress was calling imploringly for order, the Rector appeared in the doorway. (Flora Thompson)

Page 82

Between boulders and rocks crusted with shellfish and shaggy with seaweed, and past worm-channered posts that marked the fairway for fishing boats at high water, the pack hunted the otter. (Henry Williamson)

Page 83

But often enough, when the first of the month came round and I applied to him for my wage, he would only. . . . (R.L. Stevenson)

Page 83

But already, just six months later, to the astonishment of

everyone, he has become a major political figure. (Newspaper article)

Page 86

I was very uneasy and alarmed, as you may fancy, and it rather added. . . . The captain, for his part, stood staring. . . . It went sorely with all of us, I think, to leave those men. . . . I had, by this time, taken such a horror of his cruelty. . . . (R.L. Stevenson)

Pages 92–3

It stormed in the middle of the night. A flash of lightning lit up the interior of the barn, and the cows, dung heaps, and earthen pots became visible for an instant. Thunder rumbled, and a gust of wind blew open the barn door. The downpour beat on the roof like hail. The rain lashed Jacob as he closed and latched the door. He built a small fire, and sat by it praying.

After a while the wagon entered a pine-wood, which seemed less a forest than some heavenly mansion. The trees were as tall and straight as pillars, and the sky leaned on their green tops. The light which filtered through shone with all the colours of the rainbow. Jacob closed his eyes as though begrudging himself the sight of such splendour.

Wandering through the narrow street, Jacob saw how great the poverty was. Many lived in what were only dark burrows; tradesmen worked in shops that looked like kennels. A stench rose from the gutters. (Isaac Bashevis Singer)

Page 95

Macalister's boy took one of the fish and cut a square out of its side to bait the hook with. The mutilated body (it was alive still) was thrown back into the sea. (Virginia Woolf)

Page 95

In the morning they buried Mrs Collard. The serjeant got a coolie, and he dug a shallow grave. They lowered her into it covered with a blanket, and Mrs Horsefall read a little out of the Prayer Book. Then they took away the blanket because they could not spare that, and the earth was filled in. (Nevil Shute)

Page 103

The names of the authors appear in the same order as the extracts.

Daphne du Maurier: *Rebecca*; D.H. Lawrence: *The Fox*; D.H. Lawrence: *England, My England*; Barbara Cartland: *The Dream and the Glory*; Leslie Thomas: *This Time Next Week*; Ernest Hemingway: *The Old Man and the Sea*; J.R.R. Tolkien: *The Fellowship of the Ring*.

Pages 103–4

. . . . quivered like radiators in the sun. . . . the dust lifted like smoke. . . . shone into my face like a street-lamp. . . . quivering like water in the heat. . . . like diamonds scattered on velvet. . . . like a curtain nailed against the sky.